ANGRY BIRDS STAR WARS II

ULTIMATE STICKER COLLECTION

HOW TO USE THIS BOOK

READ THE CAPTIONS, THEN FIND
THE STICKER THAT BEST FITS THE SPACE.
(HINT: CHECK THE STICKER LABEL FOR CLUES!)

•

DON'T FORGET THAT YOUR STICKERS
CAN BE STUCK DOWN AND PEELED OFF AGAIN.

•

THERE ARE LOTS OF FANTASTIC EXTRA STICKERS
FOR CREATING YOUR OWN SCENES THROUGHOUT THE BOOK.

**WELCOME!
DID YOU BRING
CANDY?**

DK

LONDON, NEW YORK, MELBOURNE,
MUNICH, and DELHI

Written by Emma Grange
Edited by Hannah Dolan
Designed by Guy Harvey, Lisa Robb, and Rhys Thomas

First published in the United States
in 2013 by DK Publishing
345 Hudson Street, New York, New York 10014
10 9 8 7 6 5 4 3 2 1
001-196558-Nov/13

Page design copyright © 2013 Dorling Kindersley Limited

**MOVE OVER,
BIRD BRAIN.**

DK books are available at special discounts when purchased
in bulk for sales promotions, premiums, fund-raising, or educational use.
For details, contact:
DK Publishing Special Markets
345 Hudson Street
New York, New York 10014
SpecialSales@dk.com

A catalog record for this book is available
from the Library of Congress.

ISBN: 978-1-4654-1536-3

Color reproduction by Altaimage, UK
Printed and bound in China by L-Rex

Discover more at
www.dk.com

MEET THE NAUGHTY PIGS

Deep in space a furious fight is going on. The podgy pigs have formed an evil alliance called the Pork Federation so they can seize control of the galaxy and stuff their faces with stodgy junk food. Those angry birds had better watch out—the pigs are after them next!

PIGLATINE
This sneaky swine rules the Pork Federation. He is also known by another name—Darth Swindle—and enjoys fooling the birds while snaffling food for himself.

DARTH MOAR
The dangerous Darth Moar has a scary face and an equally scary double-bladed lightsaber weapon.

COUNT DODO
You'd never guess, but evil piggy Count Dodo used to fight on the birds' side! Piglatine persuaded him that the porky point of view is by far the best.

BRAVE BIRDS

Never fear! A flock of feathered heroes plans to save the galaxy from the scheming pigs. These birds are brave and bold, often a little bit bamboozled, and always very, very angry. Can they stop the pigs in their tracks before it's too late for everyone?

JEDI BIRDS
Some of the brave birds have special powers. They use the energy called the Force and hope to defeat the Pork Side once and for all.

R2-EGG2
Shh! R2-EGG2 has a secret. He is hiding The Egg—a mysterious object containing enough Force power to rule the entire galaxy!

C-3PYOLK

The friendly servant droid C-3PYOLK is happy to help any bird with anything they might need.

SECRET KEEPER

Yoda Bird is the Jedi Bird Master. He is the only one who knows where The Egg is hidden, but he keeps forgetting!

PECKMÉ AMIDALA

This feisty female likes to be in charge. She won't be hen-pecked by anyone, not even by her fellow birds.

RESIST THE PORK SIDE, YOU MUST... SORRY, WHERE AM I AGAIN?

ON TATOOINE

The Jedi Birds think they have found the secret to stopping the Pork Side in its thick, sticky tracks. A bird strong in the Force has just hatched on the planet Tatooine. Fortunately, the birds find Redkin Skywalker first, before the pigs can persuade him to join them instead!

YOUNG REDKIN
Does Redkin really have the powers to defeat the Pork Side? Or will he be tempted by the pigs' junk food?

BEST DROID BUDDIES
Redkin wants to know where The Egg is hidden, but he isn't about to find out. Not even C-3PYOLK knows that his friend R2-EGG2 is hiding the Force!

REDKIN'S BIGGEST FAN
Peckmé Amidala believes in Redkin Skywalker the moment she lays eyes on him. She trusts he can save the galaxy from the pigs.

JEDI BIRD MASTER

Obi-Wan Kaboomi takes Redkin under his wing and chirps him Jedi knowledge. However, he isn't sure his young apprentice is always listening.

ANGRY PIG

Piglatine sends his apprentice pig, Darth Moar, to find Redkin on Tatooine. His glaring eyes and porky snout might have scared the birds, but he arrives too late.

JABBA THE HOG

This big slimy pig hoards all the food on Tatooine for himself. Redkin is glad to leave this planet, and characters like Jabba, far behind him.

BEEP BEEP! TWEET! CHIRP!

STICK SOME STICKERS ON THIS SPREAD AND PUT A SMILE ON THESE JEDI BIRDS' FACES!

JEDI WARRIORS

The Jedi Birds are the best hope for the birds in their fight against the evil Pork Side. They are armed with lightsabers, strong in the Force, and ready to take on the pesky pigs. Can their newest recruit, the fledgling Redkin Skywalker, help them save the galaxy?

YODA BIRD
The wise old Yoda Bird is the chief bird of the Jedi roost. He is still a force to reckon with, even if he is becoming forgetful and losing all his feathers.

QUAIL-GON
This Jedi Bird is the angriest of them all. Quail-Gon has a sharp beak and an even sharper temper. He won't stand for any piggy nonsense!

STOP CHIRRUPING IN THE BACK THERE AND PAY ATTENTION, YOUNGLINGS!

MOA WINDU

This suspicious Jedi Bird is not convinced about Redkin's powers. Don't try to argue with him—Moa Windu takes everything very seriously.

OBI-WAN KABOOMI

Watch out for Obi-Wan—he is very talented, but often explodes without warning. Having received his Jedi training from Quail-Gon, Obi-Wan is now training Redkin.

REDKIN SKYWALKER

Young Redkin Skywalker is strong in the Force, but he is also impatient. Redkin wants to learn all about being a Jedi— and he wants to learn it all now!

BLUE PADAWAN

Be careful! These young Jedi Padawan Birds enjoy playing pranks. When not learning Jedi tricks, these chicks love ruffling other birds' feathers.

THE POWER OF TWO

The galaxy has seen some peculiar partnerships, some successful and some not. Pairs like Obi-Wan and Quail-Gon are stronger taking on pigs together. Meanwhile, Piglatine believes in having only one apprentice at a time. That way there are fewer pigs to steal his treats!

BIRDS OF A FEATHER
Redkin can't take his beady eyes off Queen Peckmé. She sees only the good in him, and none of his greed.

PIGLATINE'S APPRENTICE
Piglatine and his piggy pupil Darth Moar are even madder and badder together. They are both as addicted to junk food as each other!

REDKIN AND PIGLATINE
Piglatine has succeeded in poaching Redkin for the Pork Side! Redkin hopes that joining the pigs will bring him closer to finding The Egg.

FORMER JEDI BIRD
Despite being a pig, Count Dodo was once Yoda Bird's Jedi Bird apprentice! Their friendship turned to fighting when Dodo went to the Pork Side.

STOP LOOKING AT ME LIKE THAT, ARTOO. ANYONE WOULD THINK YOU'RE TRYING TO TELL ME SOMETHING!

15

DODO'S DROIDS

The crafty Count Dodo has a cunning plan. He is building an army of piggy soldiers, all programmed to serve him. These droids should inspire fear and terror in birds everywhere. If they don't, then they will have to face the anger of their commander—the fierce General Grunter!

DROID MAKER
Now that Count Dodo has joined the side of the pigs, he will do anything to defeat the birds—including building a droid army.

BATTLE PIGS
In a droid pig factory far away, something has gone wrong. These silly swines were designed to be super smart, but are easily fooled by the brainier birds.

NABOO

The planet Naboo used to be a peaceful nesting place for birds of many shapes and sizes. Now it has become a battleground as birds and pigs clash over who controls the galaxy. Can Naboo's Queen Bird Peckmé raise a fierce enough flock to scare off the invading swines?

QUEEN PECKMÉ
Naboo's Queen looks sweet and gentle, but she can get as angry as any bird. Peckmé is prepared to fight to protect her planet from the pigs.

CAPTAIN NAMAKA
This bird is the fastest flier in the galaxy! He takes his role of protecting his Queen very seriously.

JAR JAR WINGS
Jar Jar Wings has the biggest beak of all the birds and uses it for gobbling goodies. It also comes in handy for snapping at pigs!

DROID PIG ARMY

This fat battle pig army is spoiling the view on Naboo. They have orders to destroy all birds in sight.

WARRING WARHOGS

These Warhog droids are ready to roll into battle. Ready, aim—blast those birds!

JEDI BIRD ATTACK

A little bird told Quail-Gon and Obi-Wan Kaboomi that pigs were spotted on Naboo. They've flown down to fight off the intruders.

DANGEROUS DUELS

What a mess! Those angry birds are shedding feathers in their haste to launch themselves against the horrible hogs. When junk food is at stake, the greedy pigs will stop at nothing. The galaxy has seen some truly terrible one-on-one tussles as a result...

DARTH MOAR VS. QUAIL-GON
The Jedi Bird Quail-Gon is no match for Darth Moar and his double-bladed lightsaber weapon. Perhaps he can call on his feathered friend, Obi-Wan, for help?

JEDI CLASH
Redkin and Obi-Wan fight beak-to-beak when Redkin is tempted to join the pigs. Can Obi-Wan prevent his apprentice from falling to the Pork Side?

YODA BIRD VS. GRUNTER
Yoda Bird proves his powers when he duels General Grunter. Not even four lightsabers can stop the flighty Jedi Bird Master!

PIGLATINE VS. MOA WINDU
Moa Windu is not fooled by sneaky Piglatine. When he discovers the plan to tempt Redkin to the Pork Side, he swoops down to stop him.

23

BOUNTY HUNTERS

The leaders of the big, fat Pork Federation are having a hard time snuffling out their avian archenemies. If only those birds weren't so good at hiding! Luckily a few bounty hunters are on hand, willing to track down birds for a large, tasty fee.

ZAM WEASEL
Is she a pig or is she a bird? Zam Weasel may look snouty now, but she can change her appearance at any moment, making her a frightening foe.

JANGO FATT
Jango Fatt's bounty hunting fame stretches far and wide. He is loyal to the Pork Side, but only because they pay him handsomely with treats.

BOBA FATT
This little piggy looks just like his father, Jango Fatt. That's because he was copied to be just like him, then he became a bounty hunter, too.

BOUNTY HUNTERS WANTED
Pig Lords Piglatine and Lard Vader don't like to get their trotters dirty. They pay bounty hunters to do jobs—like finding birds—for them instead.

YOU CAN STICK ALL THE BOUNTY HUNTERS YOU LIKE ON HERE, THEY DON'T SCARE ME!

COPYPIGS

If some of the pigs in the massive pig army look similar, it's because they're Copypigs. These latest additions to the piggy armed forces were grown on the planet Kamino and are now ready to march into battle against the birds. Best foot forward, pigs!

ORIGINAL COPYPIG
The Pork Federation thought that Jango Fatt was such a superb pig warrior that the whole Copypig army was cloned from him.

COPYPIG ARMY
Don't try telling these pigs apart. They all look exactly the same, and are just as stupid as each other, too.

PIGFIGHTER
Lard Vader has his own personal army of Copypigs. The Pigfighters pilot the Pig Lord's spacecraft and are dressed as darkly as their evil master.

ONE, THREE, TWO, FOUR, WHO ARE WE FIGHTING FOR? THE PIG ARMY! YEAH!